Jan. 2019

DANGEROUS HOUSEHOLD ITEMS

DANGEROUS HOUSEHOLD ITEMS

DAVID ORR

COPPER CANYON PRESS
PORT TOWNSEND, WASHINGTON

Cover photo: Joe Belanger, iStock Photo

Copper Canyon Press is in residence at Fort Worden State Park in Port Townsend, Washington, under the auspices of Centrum. Centrum is a gathering place for artists and creative thinkers from around the world, students of all ages and backgrounds, and audiences seeking extraordinary cultural enrichment.

LIBRARY OF CONGRESS CATALOGING-IN-PUBLICATION DATA

Names: Orr, David, 1974– author.
Title: Dangerous household items / David Orr.
Description: Port Townsend, Washington : Copper Canyon Press, [2018]
Identifiers: LCCN 2018021079 | ISBN 9781556595479 (pbk. : alk. paper)
Classification: LCC PS3615.R588426 A6 2018 | DDC 811/.6—dc23
LC record available at https://lccn.loc.gov/2018021079

98765432 FIRST PRINTING

Copper Canyon Press
Post Office Box 271
Port Townsend, Washington 98368

www.coppercanyonpress.org

CONTENTS

I

II

III

DANGEROUS HOUSEHOLD ITEMS

I

Renovation

Sure, I'd love for you to come over.
Bring your kids if you want—there's plenty
Of space for them to run around in,
And you and I can occupy ourselves
Correcting the examples of bad taste
That persist despite my best efforts.

I haven't been here long. The last tenant,
My father, was a poor judge of color,
Not to mention an avid collector
Of velveteen cozies and plastic flamingos.
I had hoped my parents would leave me
A better legacy, but so it goes:

We all do with what we've got. Anyway,
A little work, and it should all be more
Like me, more the way I imagine myself
When I'm at my best—the most *me* me.
It's funny, though, as I was painting
The banisters this morning, I noticed

The paint was nearly thick as my finger.
It's almost like wood itself now, as if
Each rail gets larger as it gets newer,
Which I suppose it does—you don't lose
What's underneath by putting something else
On top. If I kept on painting forever

And didn't throw anything away,
I guess the rail would get thicker and thicker
Until it squeezed me right on through the wall.
I'd be just another layer then, too,
And the walls would be—inside or outside?
It's hard to say, but I can imagine

The way it would look: a thick clot of paint
Glued over with furniture, me, the walls . . .
A mess making itself bigger and bigger
Until you could see it from space, like
The Great Wall or the Mall of America.
Sometimes I think that's the way life must be,

Other times I think that's just an excuse.
Either way, we've got painting to do.
Put the phone down and hop in the car;
I've got a brush here with your name on it.

Dangerous Household Items

The only truly dangerous object
In the kitchen is the chef's knife, which sits
Point down beside the sink, held by magnets.
If you were distracted by, for instance,
Guilt, you might fumble with the handle,
Bouncing the blade off the sink's steel bottom
And into your wrist. Not deep, probably,
But another kind of distraction entirely.

The living room's hazards are limited
To the heavy oak bookshelves, and a few
Cheap and easily shattered figurines.
You'll want to look out for sorrow here,
Because a film of tears, smeared by fingers,
Might cause your reaching hand to miss
The desired crystal, pitching you into a shelf
That topples and overwhelms you. Sad, that.

And now we enter the bedroom, where light
Filters down strangely from high windows
To fall on the comforter's disturbing design
Of red and black rings in a bull's-eye.
Here, be wary of shame, which can cause
A sleeping body to sink through the center,
Arriving both reduced and concentrated
In a buried place of constant watchfulness,

A trap, almost—after which the comforter
Smoothes, reverts, restores its careful order.

Snares

Built and concealed
In so many ways
Under the rug or
Suspended from trees

Invisible lines
You felt you could trust
The seemingly solid
Undisturbed dust

You forgot yourself
And now it's over
The worst is waiting
To be discovered

Daniel

On the day we moved in, the pings, bumps, and snaps
Were scary, it's true, but probably normal;
A house accepting new patterns of weight
With protest, the way no conviction goes gently.
We laughed a little, and called it "our spirit."

Later that night, when the power conked out
And the kids were crying, the ghost got a name,
Daniel, and a history of whispered exploits,
All of them harmless, like nursery rhymes,
Or like the little fibs we tell ourselves
To explain why this or that has led to suffering.

Pretty soon, we were using him for everything.
When the Christmas tree fell, it was Daniel;
When my wife lost her ring, it was Daniel;
When the kids forgot to feed the goldfish
And it turned up dead, its eyes silvered over
Like water shadowed under sheets of ice,

Well, that became Daniel too, which was curious;
And pauses me now as I make the long walk
Down the hall to the bathroom in darkness,
And hear, in soft concert, the sound of my footfalls
Answered at once by my children's voices

Still calling to Daniel behind their door.

Inflatable Pool

Consider an object with a single purpose.
Consider the purpose not presently engaged.
Consider that the object—a child's inflated backyard pool—
Therefore ceases to draw the eye
And recedes into summer's background haze.

Consider the rain. Consider the inattention
That allows the pool to become partially filled
With rainwater. Consider the reluctance, given its newfound weight,
To attend to it. Consider subsequent rainfall,
Consequent weight increase, and further receding.

Consider the world of the inflatable pool
In its forgotten state. Consider the paradise
Its water becomes to the newly awakened embryos
Of drone flies, drain flies, beetles, and mosquitoes;
To coliforms, worms, protozoans, and nematodes.

Consider the darting, jostling, grappling
Scenes of consumption and flight; the drifting
Digestion of algae; the severed legs, ruptured membranes,
And torn-off flagella. Consider the blind appetite
That nonetheless advances a purpose. Consider the chaos

When a chipmunk, having scaled the pool's side,
Misjudges its footing and tumbles in, scrambling
Fruitlessly for purchase. Consider the end of struggle.
Consider the still surface and the twitching depths.
Consider the life. Consider the life. Consider the life.

Consider the rediscovery of the pool.
Consider the instinctive and irresistible revulsion.
Consider the lowered bucket that removes,
In a single dredging, the equivalent of an ocean.
Consider an ocean flung into the grass and dispersed.

Consider the end of this world. Consider that there is no
Grief or fear, but only forward movement
Until movement is no longer possible. Consider the lack
Of reflection and the lack of mourning for this absence.
Consider the remains. Consider these remnants.

Consider them collected in a red plastic container
And tipped into a hole beneath the sycamore.
Consider that this hole is dug with the shovel,
Which is summoned from obscurity for this purpose,
With no awareness of this purpose, and then returned

To the half-forgotten objects of the toolshed
When the hole is filled entirely with earth.

Unexpected Meeting

When he fell in the garden and cut his hand
On broken glass from the vinegar bottle
He'd thrown in drunken anger years before
(He had reached for it eagerly that night,
Mistaking it for wine in the dark kitchen),
It was no great injury, and if he felt
Amid the pain a momentary longing
To echo the longing he'd felt back then,
As you might feel stumbling on an old photo
Of yourself beside a half-forgotten person
You once were drawn to as sunflowers are drawn
Toward their namesake, which is no flower,
This quickly passed as he came to recognize
Himself at two removes, and all at once.

Sea Nettle

That it means no harm
Makes it no less painful
As it leaves a burning
Trail in its wake,

A million miniature
Bottles of poison
Slide under the skin
To tremble and break,

Their purpose served.
It will not ask
For your forgiveness.
It has moved on

To a different current.
On sensitive skin
A rash may recur
Long after the incident.

Malison

I hope someone knocks you into next week,
So that you wake to find yourself adrift
In next Monday, having missed your own birthday.

And if, by knocking you into next week,
That same person manages to send you
Into next month, then good. No paycheck for you.

Likewise, should the knocking in question occur
As the year ends, and the holidays transpire
Without you—well, welcome to January.

But most of all, I hope that you're struck
At the close of the decade's last December,
So that you rise in the cold of a new paradigm,

And, walking streets now grown unfamiliar,
Are greeted by the children of the next era
Saying they remember you. And that you've aged.

The Chameleon

Alone among the superheroes,
He failed to keep his life in balance.
Power Man, the Human Shark—they knew
To hold their days and nights in counterpoise,
Their twin selves divided together,
As a coin bears with ease its two faces.

Not so the Chameleon. He was
Too many things to count, and was counted on
To be too many things. When he came to grief,
As was perhaps inevitable,
His body was overlooked for hours,
Having been pressed by force of habit

Into the likeness of what had killed him.

Tea

The cup lay deserted on the table.
The tea leaves smoldered in the cup.
The leaves smoldered and transformed the water
Into naked expressions of tea

And impassioned expressions of tea
And bitter expressions of tea.
The tea became displeasing to its maker
As it became increasingly itself.

The Heroine

She had always been special
And had resented it since childhood:
The signs, the portents, the wondrous
And irritating talking animals,
The flowers that sang her name
Like a hymn in the local Home Depot,
And worst of all, the misfit friends
With their sad quirks and barely disguised
Fear of the figure she would become.
Her life, she felt, was an endless rehearsal
From the same shopworn script
Filled with tedious quips and second-tier villains.

Nonetheless, it was her story and her duty.
When the great moment finally came,
The vague horror at last embodied,
She faced the trials, resisted the temptations
Of power, wealth, and erotic bliss,
And followed the guidance of the local druid,
Who marked the path to the final battle
From a storm drain near the Olive Garden,
Just to the right of Joe's Tacos.
She entered, and after a long struggle,
Defeated her evil counterpart
With a swift *riverso*. The town was saved,

The world was saved. But what of her?
The flowers made her an honorary rose.
The druid named her a guardian spirit.
The misfits called her their coolest friend.
"Fuck you," she said, and got on a train.
She passed through endless miles of strip malls,
And in time arrived at a city—*the* city—

Sometimes mentioned in the script's margins
As a place people came from or went to.
It existed in fact. There were Fiats and Kias,
And luxury taxes, and thirty-year mortgages,
And warehouses leased by Internet retailers,

One of which gave her a temporary job
Folding and sorting pants. Her days were spent
With bootcuts, khakis, slims and skinnies,
Culottes, corduroys, crops, and low-rises,
Arriving in crates from China or Indonesia,
And all bound to be worn and discarded.
Her hands passed over them, under them,
Dipping into the dusty ocean of fabric
And finding no single story there, but rather
So many stories that events became
Rendered liquid, each moment part of
A larger moment forever washing over her,

Washing back and forth over her forever,
As if she were a small, tide-pool creature,
Made to savor or suffer with each passing wave.
The water filled her, the water left her.
She was nobody, she was everybody.

Quarters

Ramón was the Magician's assistant,
At least until the boss could find a woman,
Some beauty queen able to work the panels
With Ramón's always impeccable timing.
"She'll have big tits, Ramón," said the Magician,
"And an ass like a peach, just wait and see."

But no one like that would ever come along.
The Magician was old; he owed money.
And while his remarkable profession
Attracted women, they were pale, hungry girls,
Restless for handcuffs and invisible keys.
It was a lonely life of birthday parties.

When the children's faces turned, expectant,
The Magician would savor the words of release,
As red scarves shrouded the silver chalice.
His oldest trick, yet still miraculous,
As out of nothing it seemed he drew forth life,
And real life paused to wonder. One second. Two.

And the white bird flew!

Then back to earth, back to himself,
Back to the back of the room and a check,
Back to Ramón, and an inscrutable nod;
And finally, back to the alcove studio,
Where the mirror reflects a prefab bookcase,
Its paperbacks sorted by subject and author,

And the small bed waits with its nylon sheets,
The bed so tightly, so carefully made
That the Magician sometimes, to please himself,
Would bounce upon it the very same quarter
That hours before had become incarnate
Where nothing had dwelt in Ramón's empty hands.

Recycling

Newspapers, magazines, and glossy inserts
May be combined with other paper types,
But plastic bags, product samples, and shrink-wrap
Must be isolated for individual disposal.

Clean corrugated boxes and egg cartons
Are acceptable, as are pamphlets and cookbooks,
But wax- or plastic-coated boxes should be left
Beside gift bags and wedding invitations,

Where they will be periodically inspected,
And, if approved, cleaned and restored,
Albeit in the desultory manner in which one
Does favors for former lovers. Opened mail

And nonmetallic stationery and cards
Are permitted, unless the messages they contain
Involve condolences, gratitude, or threats,
In which case they must be sealed in airtight bags.

The bags must then be placed in containers
With labels indicating the nature of the contents
And the intensity—for example, genuine regret
Receives a red check mark, whereas regret laced

With schadenfreude would receive a black X.
Unpostmarked letters addressed to "you"
Must be placed in a blue bin, unless the salutation
Is followed by a cliché, truism, or old joke,

Which requires a bag sealed inside another bag
And placed sideways in the appropriate bin.
Unaddressed, unpostmarked letters or diary pages
Implying that one's inner life is determined

By a series of breakages, differing in their specifics
But resembling one another in ferocity,
Each of which appears to leave one arrested in time,
So that by early middle age, we are presented

With a series of selves frozen in tableau,
As if a life were a mountain upon which
A train of hikers had expired in the cold,
Each hiker being distinguishable from the others

Only by virtue of positioning and the aging process,
Must go in the gray bin, clearly labeled,
Along with letters that reference previous letters,
And scripts that break the fourth wall,

Particularly in the service of brittle cleverness.
Those that do so out of desperation
Or an almost pitiable effort to connect
When it is far too late, and so improbable

As to be nearly impossible, as in Jane Austen's
Persuasion, which, as she surely knew,
Was no less a fantasy for being described as such,
May be placed in metal cans with napkins,

Along with mirrors from which the reflective backing
Has become detached, making the mirror
More accurately described as a window
Through which images pass but do not return,

Such images being the reverse of those
Captured in photographs of solitary figures,
Which are nothing but a perpetual returning
And must be isolated for individual disposal,

Unless the figure is positioned such that
The illusion of a connecting gaze is maintained,
That is, the subject's eyes follow the viewer,
Which is a function of the mind's perception

Of pictorial space as independent of the visual field
That contains it, allowing the illusion to be
Maintained despite rotation of the frame
And consequent "thinning" of the figure,

In which case the photograph may be sealed
In an airtight bag and placed in a red bin,
Which should be left beside the green bin
That contains electronic storage devices

Whose circuitry retains documentation
Of individuals once central to the owner
Who have vanished or become diminished,
And who exist now as purely digital presences,

Rendering them weightless though not formless,
And still somehow dense with meaning, like obelisks
Rising alongside an ancient road and inscribed
With markings untranslatable yet vaguely sad,

And that circuitry must be clearly separated
From any corporeal residue, hair or nail clippings,
Which are not acceptable, although drawings
In which figures are merged with landscapes

Are acceptable if the landscapes in question
Involve harvestable terrain, and not,
For example, ice floes or snow-caked tundra
In which one could imagine a body eventually

Becoming as alien as stone or iron or plastic,
Though recoverable for study by future generations.
Bodies so discovered are acceptable
And will be picked up by 3:30 on weekdays,

Along with newspapers, magazines, and glossy inserts.

Kindness

White and bland, it pools
And pools until one sinks. It
Drowns the cry for help,
And yet one drinks it.

Sorrow

Its place is not
in desert heat
or extremities
of frozen seas
but rather on
untroubled lawns
awash with flowers
all the years
the petals falling
short of filling
the yellow, bare
outlines where
some activity
used to be.

Beach Reading

When Travis McGee's friend Meyer
Lent his boat to his niece, Norma,
And her new husband, Evan,
He never dreamed he was signing
Their death warrant.

For suddenly,
Out in the waters of the Florida Keys,
The boat was destroyed
By an explosion.

To all appearances, only Norma, Evan,
And a crew member were aboard
When it happened. But
Travis McGee begins to suspect
It's not that simple.

It is never that simple
When Travis McGee sets out to solve
A mystery. It is never a matter
Of being in the wrong place
When a series of unrelated

Phenomena interact
To calamitous effect,
As with most fatal illnesses,
Or as when, above an airstrip,
A flock of geese pours

Into a turbine. No, there will be
An intention that demands
Further investigation,
And Travis McGee will set out
On a solitary quest

Joined at times by companions
With certain virtues,
Yet generally expendable,
To find a culprit whose guilt will not
Be shaken by subsequent events,

As might happen if it were
Discovered the boat had been
Diverted by a stray current
Into a branch that, striking Evan,
Propelled his lit cigarette

Into an open gas tank,
Leading to the explosion at issue,
And startling a nearby flock of geese
That swerves abruptly
Toward a plane whose plunge

Terminates in a facility
Producing the only medicine
That can save a dying man—
The author's father, let us say—
Leaving the entire scenario

Clouded in vague forms of smoke
Shrouded in vague forms of smoke
That will not appear
In the narrative at hand, in which
There are no geese and no one is

Holding a cigarette,
And the author does not, and I do not
Have a collection of my father's old
Shirts haunting my closet
And all along, see,

It was the crewman.

The Frog

Eight years after the fact I find
In my father's old bag a silver frog,
A trinket the size of a luggage key,
Its function lost in obscurity,

Like a relic from some vanished tribe
Whose name is no longer even a name.
My daughter joins it with her toys.
What are you playing? I ask. *A game.*

Fable

On the boy's fifth birthday, his father gave him a lion.
"This is not," said the father, "a symbolic lion;
It's a real lion, and will require real care."
The boy could see that this must be true,
Because the lion already had pissed on the carpet.
So he undertook the burden of the beast
Reluctantly, knowing it wouldn't be light.

Soon, however, the lion became part of his life.
In the woods beside the soccer fields
Where the boy mostly failed to score,
The lion paced or, more often, slept and quietly farted.
In school it was a dim, golden presence;
Sometimes close at hand (at lunch, for example);
Other times, unaccountably difficult to locate,
As when the boy was being pushed or made fun of.

The boy grew older; the lion remained the same.
Fresh from the triumph of collegiate sex,
The boy met the lion's yellow gaze in the bathroom mirror.
"Don't you have somewhere else to be?" the boy asked.
To which the lion said nothing, being a lion.
As the boy grew into manhood, the years blurred
With wife and children and the hopeful sheen
Of household devices. The lion slept outside sometimes,
But could still be counted on to reemerge
At sunrise, its pelt lit softly by the warming sky,
To take a dump, or simply flop on the driveway.

Then the boy's father became ill, as all of us must.
He was trundled about and filled with cisplatin
And drugs to relieve the side effects of cisplatin,
And drugs to relieve the side effects of those drugs,

But nothing was availing. On the last night,
The boy sat alone beside him, for it was his turn
To keep the vigil. There was no special sign
As death came on, but when the boy looked up,
He saw that the lion had crossed the threshold.

"It's okay," he told the lion. "I know what you have to do."
And so the lion ate the body of the boy's father.
It was not symbolic. The boy was surprised
By how much blood his father's body still contained,
And disturbed, as he realized what a rude business
A lion's dinner really was. Then it was over,
And night didn't swallow the room, but it did get dark.

The boy waited, and the lion sat silently, tail twitching.
And suddenly, as if a great wave had passed over him,
The boy realized he was waiting
For nothing, that he had been waiting for nothing
For hours, that he had been waiting for nothing
For years, that he had always been waiting for nothing,
And that he was in a room with a lion.

He backed away slowly and slipped out the door,
Only to see his mother hurrying down the hall,
Having been alerted by the nurses,
And moving slightly behind her, entirely at ease,
The warm orange glow of a tiger.

Sandbox

My child puts her hands
Into the sand with the hands
Of other children, whose hands
Are warm from the hands
Of other parents, and the sand
Is no longer merely sand
But a small history of sand
As translated by the sand
In this particular playground,
As now the background
Of hands, sand, and ground
Rises into the foreground,
And my child's small form
Blurs with the larger form
Of children drawing form
From the sand's formless form
And I want it to stop.
I want the blurring to stop,
For my child's image to stop
Eroding in sand that won't stop
Covering itself in itself
As if it had forgotten itself
And had to repeat itself
In order to maintain itself.

The Source

Everyone ought to be something,
So my aunt did her best to trace
A path back over the mountains
To find the family's source.

"It's pretty hard to figure out,
Since most of them could only talk."
She meant the records—deeds and such—
Were signed with nothing but an X,

Which could have been anyone.
So she got as far as Darlington
And a marriage license,
Then drew a blank, an emptiness.

That couple stands with nothing
Behind them, as best we can tell,
Yet still across our lives they throw
Their blinding shadow.

Graphology

As a man will sit in a day-bright diner
To clear his head in the middle of the night,
So I'll flip the switch on the bedside lamp
Whenever I dream I've seen your face.

And nothing's there. But that doesn't matter;
It's the clarity that counts. If light
Shines on nothing, it shines nonetheless,
And argues that how we see is how we think,

And how we think is who we are. That's clear
As the world at the height of afternoon,
Or the words I've written on this notepad,
The words we could send to a man tomorrow,

Who would claim to find my truest meaning
In the way I dot my i's and cross my t's.

Homestretch

If you were lost,
And needed finding,
And happened to be
An Ancient Greek,
Good luck meant stumbling
Onto Proteus,
The oldest and wisest
God of the Sea,
Whose mind was singular
As the ocean,
But whose body shuffled
Like a swell
From this to that.

*

How unlucky, though, to stumble on
   Not Proteus, but his lost twin brother
Who matched the Sea God in reverse;
   His flesh block-solid as an anvil,
His mind a current changing course
   At every turn; each face, each gesture
Dislodging what had gone before
   In ripples lost inside themselves.

He couldn't know, he couldn't name
   His own name, much less steer you home;
And who could reach inside his head
   To free him from that freedom?

*

The last time he knew something was wrong,
That is, before everything went wrong,
We were outside and it was nighttime.
During dinner, he had twice forgotten my name.
He said something about it, and I nodded,
Not sure what it was I was nodding to,
As from far away inside his house
The old man's TV noisily announced
The victory, after five hundred laps,
Of Dale Earnhardt, or maybe of Dale Earnhardt Jr.

Backmasking

When you played the record backward,
Everything that was supposed to happen
Changed, and your perspective changed,
As words became sounds, and sounds became
Changed, and your perspective changed
Everything that was supposed to happen
When you played the record backward.

Fata Morgana

The three principle forms of mirage—
Inferior, superior, and Fata Morgana—
All depend on the inversion of an object,
Literally the mirroring of an object
("Mirage" stems from the Latin *mirare,*
"To look at," which in turn derives
From *mirari,* "to wonder at"), and are
Distinguished by the nature of this mirroring,
Whether, for instance, the image appears
Below the object itself (an inferior mirage),
Or above it (superior), or in combination
And distorted—elongated, compressed,
And rapidly changing—as is the case
With the rare and peculiar Fata Morgana,
Which takes its name from Morgan Le Fay,
King Arthur's mysterious half sister,
Who serves as enemy, savior, or lover
To her brother, depending on the chronicle,
And whose magic governed shadowed Avalon
And its shadow versions of humanity—
Le Fay means "the fay," or "the fairy"—
And one can see how early viewers
Of the Fata Morgana would indeed
Have supposed the phenomenon revealed
A fairy kingdom, a many-tiered castle
Shifting at the skyline with alien elegance
And promising a half-longed-for communion,
Which is, of course, the standard portrayal
Of mirages—that is, as things wished for
But unobtainable, and unobtainable
Because ultimately nonexistent—
And why we associate the mirage with
Delusion rather than simple misperception,

Such that when we say a feeling or belief
Was a "mirage," we mean we were deceived
Not as to its nature, but its possibility:
A mirage is simply not there, much as
A fantasy has no underlying substance
(One can have a fantasy *about* something
Or someone real, but the vision itself
Is purely fictional), though this notion
Is incorrect or at least inaccurate
With respect to actual mirages, which are
Genuine reflections of physical facts:
From certain vantage points, there is no way
Not to see a Fata Morgana, as it results
From the bending of light rays along
A temperature inversion and is therefore
Unaffected by any effort the viewer makes
To see through it, and can even be
Photographed, unlike an optical illusion,
Yielding blue-gray blocks or thin blue ribbons
Rising and sinking as if slowly drawn
By hidden forces through the thickening liquid
Of which they are themselves composed,
An effect best seen in time-lapse video,
In which the strange, estranging spectacle
Can be disconcerting much as a person
Can seem disconcerting in those moments
In which we suddenly perceive the extent
To which we have failed to perceive them,
Neither as they understand themselves, nor
As they "truly are," which is to say,
As some imaginary observer with perfect
Perspective might label or describe them,
And it is as if we had discovered
In the middle of a private conversation
That there was no conversation, but rather

That the object of our address had been
Responding to cues from some other,
Indiscernible speaker or theater, and what
We had believed to be behavior
Answering our own requests had been
Something closer to coincidence, as if
We were children whose cry of "Run away!"
Overlapped with a cartoon character's choice
To flee from a threat, and this knowledge
Blows through us like cold wind across some vast
And yet imprisoning plain, and should we run
Or stand still, we can't decide, and the landscape
Abruptly skews around us, as cliffs
Rise from what had once been stable ground,
And black oceans drown the landmarks
By which we hoped to navigate, the ice
Ascending in mountains like the mountains
That faced Sir John Ross in 1818,
The mountains that rose from the terminus
Of the Lancaster Sound in serried ranks,
Obscuring the true fact of open waters
That would have led to the Northwest Passage,
The mountains so real he gave them a name,
The Croker range, after John Croker,
The First Secretary of the Admiralty,
A decision he would look back upon
As one of the thousand branching paths
He should have forgone, as his belief
That the way ahead was blocked would result
In humiliation when the peaks were proved,
Only a year later, and by his former mate,
To be a Fata Morgana, and yet even so,
Had he possessed a sufficient telescope,
He would have seen only mountains
Growing out of mountains, and trees

Merging with their own upper branches
To produce yet larger trees, and perhaps,
Though no human figure could emerge
From that distorted land, a solitary bear
Standing erect on its hind legs would be
Elongated, compressed, and rapidly changed
To become something almost human,
Something adjoining the idea of human,
Though far too large and strange for comfort,
And be given a name by Ross and his crew
As it turned and changed, as it grew and moved
As if in response to some unheard call.

Appetites

I store them just outside of town
In a barn I hold by dubious title.
They rest among abandoned tools
And shy, trespassing animals.

Swamp Fox

The trick is to come out of nowhere,
To emerge from the mist, the smoke,
The trees, the undergrowth,
As if you had always been the character
Upon whom the final act must turn.

The trick is for there to be no visible
Process, no development,
No chain of events that might be traced
To a decision made long ago, coming
Resolutely home as if by gravity.

The trick is to convince the world
That one doesn't exist, that the river
Wasn't channeled, the match not dropped,
The road never opened, much less taken,
And the piano now falling

Only by accident from the thirteenth floor.

The Train

Not that anyone will care,
But as I was sitting there

On the 8:07
To New Haven,

I was struck by lightning.
The strangest thing

Wasn't the flash of my hair
Catching on fire,

But the way people pretended
Nothing had happened.

For me, it was real enough.
But it seemed as if

The others saw this as nothing
But a way of happening,

A way to get from one place
To another place,

But not a place itself.
So, ignored, I burned to death.

Later, someone sat in my seat
And my ashes ruined his suit.

The Abduction

For all that vanished week, he seemed to float
In bath-warm water by a harmless beach,
Never noticing the spinning instruments
That exposed his spine, nor the probes that ran
Along his lower vertebrae like mice.
Later, he would wake each night screaming
In helpless confusion, but at the time
There was just the sun, the beach, the sun, the salt water,
And dark forms being kind.
                                          Only a month
After the incident, having lost the skill
Of knowing what was real, he walked
Into headlights he had thought were his wife.

Against Strange Maladies a Sovereign Cure

In the middle, before we learned the truth,
My sister Ruth and I were tucked in bed,
Burning like torches. Mary would enter,
With pitchers of water and bowls of ripe fruit,
And fuss as if we were her own true daughters.
(Our mother, fearing the sickness, had left
Us in the care of servants, as seemed best.)

When Ruth passed on, I barely knew—the fever
Had turned the room to a flickering haze.
Yet even so, I remember Mary's face
Collapsing in waves as she changed the sheets.
As young as I was, I couldn't foresee
A grief like that; it almost seemed frightening:
As if she herself, and not Ruth, had died.

At the time, I thought no greater love
Could be found in this world; that her devotion
Recalled, in its way, the spirit of God,
Who asks no more than our fondest embrace,
Yet for this would sacrifice anything,
Not sparing the tenderest parts of himself—
Though perhaps that is a poor example,

For you know the rest of the story:
The lone Inspector's knock, Mary's arrest,
And the teams of nervous workers arriving
To burn each thing she had touched or breathed on,
Including the food she prepared that morning.
They had lost her trail, but found it again
When news of my sister reached the paper.

How much she knew, or guessed, I'll never know;
Regardless, my recovery from fever
Was slow; my sleep troubled by memories
Of Ruth, of Mary, of a bowl of ripe apples
Arranged with care, then fed to the fire.

Water

At home at any table,
It partners any dish
From bitter dandelions
To force-fed flesh,

And needs no special cup
Or silver heirloom tray;
It fills its place however
That place is made,

And has no expectations.
All settings are all right.
It doesn't judge your cutlery
Or appetite.

It doesn't judge at all,
Not criminals or kings,
Or starving settlers snowbound
And considering.

The King

It was a sad day in the imagination
When they brought the tyrannosaur in for judgment.
He had been surpassed, all agreed,
By gigantosaurus, spinosaurus,
And now was thought by many experts
To be merely a scavenger, no tyrant at all.

"But I have killed," he cried, "I have murdered,
And felt nothing but pleasure in the act.
When in your mind you moved like a brush fire
Across the landscape, taking what you liked,
It was my form, my fire, that you borrowed,
And my spirit that tore the neighbor, claimed his home,
And savaged his long-coveted wife
Despite her tears and the small child looking on.
I am the shotgun, the hatchet, the sharpened thumbnail;
Like salt or lye, I poison the very ground;
I am the dream of wanting made fact,
And I will not end until the world ends."

In a monarch's fury he raised the tiny arms
That have puzzled science and amused moviegoers,
But it was no use: The court was rational,
His arguments mere figuration,
And he was taken away like an average person,
To be processed, to be put into the system.

Invasive

The small Asian
mongoose will
dispossess
cobras, yes,
and rats, of course,
but much less
renowned is his
taste for birds
and bird eggs;
when introduced
to new neighbors,
great or small,
he studiously
subdues them all
to build his race
of tiny czars,
leading to fables
of fearlessness from
English writers
but in the groves
of Puerto Rico a
disconcerting
absence of nightjars.

The Big Bad

At last we decoded the terminal message,
Only to find the pattern we had expected
Was false—a false trail of false bread crumbs
Designed to leave pitfalls undetected.

We found a new pattern. We found a hand
Moving pieces we had thought were only
Part of the board, and shifting them to vantage points
We had ignored. We rewrote the battle plan

And reconfigured the satellite array
To show our progress from the very beginning.
The fault should be traceable—and hence correctable—
And once we found it, we'd be winning.

We found a new pattern. We followed its track
To a forest beside an abandoned tunnel
Diving wide as a boxcar into the rock.
A stale breeze blew over rusting shovels

And all of our instruments confirmed a hit.
We set a perimeter. We sent in a scout.
From the interior, nothing looked back at us.
No tracks indicated a force had come out.

But we had a pattern. At dawn, we dispatched
A team of our best, our trackers and stone killers,
To see if the signals were finally a match
And, if so, to counterattack. And now we wait.

And now we wait. The tunnel gives nothing back.
The trees are revealing the first signs of gold
But the air is unmoving. The air is still.
It is quiet here, and getting cold.

Cheney in Italy

In the epilogue, Mr. Cheney writes that after undergoing
heart surgery in 2010, he was unconscious for weeks. During
that period, . . . he had a prolonged, vivid dream that he was
living in an Italian villa, pacing the stone paths to get coffee
and newspapers.

New York Times, August 24, 2011

My dream reminds me of a poem,
A thing half in light, half in shadow,
And richer somehow than daily life,
Like life as overlaid with bronze
And warmed by slow internal fires.
And like a poem, it's always the same:
I'm getting coffee and a newspaper.
The newspaper, I know, will be in English,
Though the people I meet don't speak it.
"*Ciao,*" they say. "*Buon giorno.*"
I nod and smile; they understand, or seem to.

Now I'm sitting on a bench. The paper
Is covered with names: Syria, Iran,
Manama, Quetta, Kandahār, al-Faw . . .
The names are beautiful, removed from sentences,
And I imagine them as birds lighting briefly
On this or that branch of a massive tree,
Whose crown is all afire with sunlight
But whose dark roots are reaching for water
To keep to themselves. The church bells ring,
And a woman grins and leans from a windowsill,
Exposing pale moons of skin. I smile

And look away, over the hills to the vineyards.
There's something I ought to remember,
But it's hard to concentrate inside this dream.

I find myself saying something about coffee
In a language I didn't know I spoke.
The coffee tastes like almonds and ashes,
And I know the hilltops are covered with ashes,
Even from here. It's as if my body
Were the land itself, and the land's people,
And I feel myself responding to them
As I would to my own family, to myself,

And this is how I know I'm dreaming.
The world turns and is turned by advantage;
My neighbor wants my home, my land,
And his desire constructs the system
That is itself absorbed by other systems,
All intertwined in ways that are beautiful
As a body is beautiful, or a forest, or a name—
An infinitely complex thing made simple.
The leader's job is to see this simplicity,
To reduce each thing to its useful essence.
He is an artisan, never an artist;
What he makes has always been made before.

The wind rises, and I hear far-off singing,
The syllables blending to one utterance
I can almost taste. I reach for a pastry,
Which is a *pastry,* not an assortment
Of flour and sugar, milk and measurements,
Varying and impure. Truth leaves things out, leaves
Parts out to construct the memorable whole
To which we give a proper name. The names
Are what matter and persist. And I think
Of the poem by Frost, one of few I recall,
In which truths are things we return to
As they fall in and out of fashion.
There are dunes in the poem, and blowing wind.
The truths are covered and uncovered.

But what if there is only the one truth,
That is not obscured by sand, nor hidden away
In a remote valley, distant from those
Who might harm it, or whom it might harm;
What if there is only one truth lying darkly
At the bottom of the sea, waiting to rise
And overturn the cliffs that protect us?
Clouds pass over the sun; the bronze dims.
My bench looks out on miles and miles of railway
Looping into the hills through trees and quiet ashes,
Spiraling away into the sky or sea beyond.

A train is coming, I know it's mine.
As it nears the station, gleaming like ink,
I see it trails vast banks of clouds,
Clouds bruised upon clouds. The man beside me
Checks his watch and seems unconcerned.
I realize I need to tell him something
About truth, or dreams—but the train is here.

South Tower

From ten floors down and across the street,
The surprise, he said, was really the paper—
The thousands and thousands of sheets of paper
Whipping and pausing and flipping side to side,
Pressing against the glass then falling away
Like a flock of white birds gone crazy and dying.
The phone he held was suddenly unfamiliar,
As one sheet paused before him for an instant:
A firm header, a block of text, and below,
A photo, or maybe a corporate sigil
That he could almost but not quite make out.

Found Poem

I didn't know where to put this
So I'll just post it here.
The one thing that bugged me
Was that corpses disappear.

It doesn't give the right feeling
When you kill someone
And their corpse turns into glowing
Dust or a pile of bones.

Of course if you clear out a place
And new inhabitants move in
Corpses shouldn't still be there
But you get the idea.

I feel fewer and fewer games
Have corpses after kills.
Is it because of memory?
If so, they should use less memory.

Give us bloody floors,
Bloody walls
And cut up corpses
Filling the room!

The war was a good example of this,
It was too clean afterward.
Would have made a huge impact
If the place were filled with death—

That would make it a true dark fantasy.
What do you guys think? Agree or disagree?

Victory

Lepisosteus osseus

Despite it all, something stirs at the sight
Of the cool, enameled body,
The unreflecting eye,
And the long jaw like a chisel
With its single, violent purpose.

It hangs dead-still at the water's surface
And seems lifeless, until
A flickering gesture
Carves fish after fish
From any school that swims too close

And creates in the world a new absence,
As if this might be the shaper
As well as the defacer
Of the damaged masterpiece
Whose headless body hails the bodies

Of the many Egyptians excised at Cyprus.

Time's Arrow

The funniest thing about the day
That time ran backward for half an hour
Was not, as you might suppose, the newborns
Leaping up into their mothers' bellies,
Or the corpses getting briefly sick.

Nor was it the sellers becoming buyers,
Or the writers becoming censors,
Or the shrieks dissolving into silence
As everywhere aches were soothed
With kicks and punches from the bloody-minded.

No, the funniest thing about that day
Was the half a world that slept in darkness,
Not knowing if the dreams they dreamed
Were false—how could they?—but grateful, regardless,
Should the dream of falling become the dream of flying.

Cardenio

In the great lost play *Cardenio*
The rising action never falls,
The end is always never-ending;
Somewhere in Spain, the curtain calls

Go on and on and on and on
And on, as if to signify
That stories that are never told
Are stories that can never die,

Just as lovers who can never quite
Connect are frozen in the pose
Of wanting, reaching, turning to
The thing that, rising, never rose.

And though we'll never realize
What all the talking could have meant,
The characters we might have been
Still come and go, and came and went.

Edinburgh

The obsolescent
And frequently wet
Walls of this castle—
Museum, really—
Can still manage
On certain nights
(As on the few nights
I spent with you)
A glamour one is
Almost fooled by.

Songbook

i. "In a Big Country"

In a big country, dreams stay with you.
But in a small country, or worse,
A small country inside a big country,
They leave without warning. The letters
Arrive from increasingly remote locales,
Smelling of oranges and allspice,
Stained with unpronounceable wines.

Still doing great. You would not believe
The birds here. Hope all's well! Too bad
How things worked out. Have met
The most interesting screenwriter.

Within a month, you find yourself
Misplacing the letters, and from there
It's a short step to burning them.
There's a steady glow in the backyard
Of the small country's smallest house,
And a frozen tower of ash that lingers
Until one day, a door opens in the smoke

And out steps a familiar form,
Smelling of oranges, sporting a tan.

ii. "Just Like Heaven"

Show me how you do that trick,
The one with the box, the one
In which the box is transformed
Into a transformative vessel
And split in half, allowing
The entity contained within
To continue moving as if whole,
To continue as though undamaged,
As if choice did not require division,
But allowed continuity across all
Possible universes, implying
That there is only one universe,
Or perhaps there is no universe
In which I did not think
Of you constantly, and want not to.

iii. "Don't You (Forget About Me)"

Love's strange, so real in the dark,
And then less real as the sun rises,
So that by noon, it's mostly a memory
And mostly a false one, a case

Of déjà vu, or perhaps jamais vu,
A familiar thing grown suddenly unfamiliar,
As when an image or word is repeated—
Love love love love love love love—

Such that the word ceases to seem
Like a word at all, and becomes instead
A sudden door on a strange hillside,
A door it would be perilous to open,

If only because having entered,
You must someday leave, and having left,
You can never forget.

iv. "The Song Remains the Same"

Everything that's small has to grow
As a matter of law in that country,
A clear rule that nonetheless leaves
Certain questions unresolved
Regarding the increase or intensification
Of negative or reductive qualities.

For instance, they felt themselves to be
At the end of a road no longer a road
And barely even a path. The sky that had once
Expanded as if blown by a child's laughter
Now pressed down as if to sink
Through their bodies to fill the very earth.

The sky pressed. The sky pressed through.
They felt themselves become smaller and smaller
As it grew and grew and grew.

Folly

I was at loose ends, neither here nor there,
And it seemed like easy work—lend a hand
With a three-day demolition project
On the county's mostly empty east side.
I pictured a barn, already half knocked down
By decades of snow and trespassing ice,
A sight you might catch from a passing train
And think on idly before your phone rings,
Blending the vision with hundreds just like it
As standard scenery, meaning nothing.

I was wrong. What stretched before us and rose
Over us (it sprawled atop a rocky knoll)
Was as if a farmhouse had exploded
And reformed as a funhouse-mirror portrait.
There were porches over porches, a gate
That opened onto nothing but a gate,
And ladders climbing to, I swear, a turret
Whose crenellation was crazed and glittering
With bits of aluminum, plastic, glass,
And steel plates etched with something like writing.
It clung to that ground but seemed unearthly.

We stood there awhile looking at the thing
As you might look on a person caught unawares
Inspecting his body. The foreman coughed.
"We got to aim the bulldozer just right."
I said that for all we could tell out front
The whole place might be filled with dynamite.
"It's not," he said, "but you go look around."
So I did. And the time inside seems strange now—
I'm told it was only an hour or so,
Yet each scene holds the silvered clarity

So often absent from ordinary life,
Yet present in rare moments of upheaval.

You have to understand it was organized.
The kitchen was plain but tidy, the shelves straight.
There was no chaos of stray belongings
Proclaiming a life gone past the horizon.
But there was an application of method
That knew no boundaries. Thousands and thousands
Of coins made a constellation on one wall,
Each one labeled with a painted character;
And rooms gave way to rooms, each added
According to some unknowable plan
And adorned with collections, arrangements
Of nails and pens, of shells and wood carvings
Suggesting a story they couldn't tell.

It was the work of a man, I could see,
And there must have been a point to it at first—
Something to do with a woman, maybe,
Though nothing to do with a real woman—
But he had become his own audience,
And in trying to be two things at once,
Performer and applauder, lover and loved,
Had made something for neither. A memory
Had never gotten worked in or smoothed out,
And that one disruption caused wild spirals
That now stretch and stretch and stretch and stretch
As if to embrace the world, yet instead
Hold the world at an awkward hand's-length distance—
Going through it, I would not have wanted
To see my own face, nor to catch the eyes
Of the men standing curious beside me.
We looked down and away from one another,
At our phones or into the creeping myrtle.

Well, the job ended up taking a week.
Some of the guys said we'd never get it all,
And yet in the end there was nothing left.

Winter

The gravest season
And least understood
Is more than pale heads
In fur hoods

More than the blackbirds
No longer singing
Above the clearing they are
Darkly ringing

More than the snow
Embodied as men
Posed in solitary
Vigil again

And equals the need
To live past recalling
Out where the mercury
Won't stop falling

Acknowledgments

I'm grateful to the following journals, in which several of these poems first appeared: *Narrative, The New Yorker, Pleiades, Poetry,* and *The Yale Review.*

My thanks also to Michael Wiegers, Laura Buccieri, Emily Grise, John Pierce, and everyone at Copper Canyon Press, as well as to Phil Kovacevich for designing the book and to Alison Lockhart and David Caligiuri for their meticulous copyediting.

About the Author

David Orr is the poetry columnist for the *New York Times Book Review* and teaches at Rutgers University. A native South Carolinian, he lives in Princeton, New Jersey.

Poetry is vital to language and living. Since 1972, Copper Canyon Press has published extraordinary poetry from around the world to engage the imaginations and intellects of readers, writers, booksellers, librarians, teachers, students, and donors.

WE ARE GRATEFUL FOR THE MAJOR SUPPORT PROVIDED BY:

THE PAUL G. ALLEN
FAMILY FOUNDATION

The Chinese character for poetry is made up of two parts:
"word" and "temple." It also serves as pressmark for
Copper Canyon Press.

The poems are set Adobe Garamond Pro.
The headings are in Trade Gothic.
Book design and composition by Phil Kovacevich.